Learn to Read Phonetically Collection 1

Short Vowels and Single Consonants

Written and Illustrated by

Gloria Torres, Mark Torres, and Theresa Torres
Edited by Nicholas Torres

Collection 1: This is a collection of six stories written with <u>single consonants</u> and short vowels only. The first three stories are written with the *Dolch phonetic short vowel and single consonant sight words. The second three stories incorporate other short vowel single consonant words. Each story has a list of vocabulary words at the beginning as well as questions to answer at the end. These stories were illustrated with colored pencils, watercolor paints, and cutouts.

*The 315 Dolch Sight Vocabulary list is taken from the Picture Word Cards and Popper Words Set 1 (included in item #0-07-609422-7), plus Popper Words Set 2 (#0-07-602539-X) published by SRA (1-888-SRA-4543 or SRAonline.com).

NEXT BOOK

Collection 2: This will be a collection of four stories that continue to use short vowel and single consonant words with the addition of <u>s added to nouns and verbs and 's added to indicate possession</u>. Each story will have a list of vocabulary words at the beginning as well as questions to answer at the end.

DEDICATION

These stories are dedicated to our parents for helping us learn to read and encouraging us to draw. It is also dedicated to our cousins who read our stories with enthusiasm.

ACKNOWLEDGMENTS

These books were created for *Schuler Phonics Second Part*, authored by Mary M. Schuler. This collection includes companion stories #1-6.

It is highly recommended that BEFORE reading this book, your child/student should study the following sections in <u>Schuler Phonics Second Part Vowel Reference Card</u> by Mary M. Schuler:

1. Single Consonants with Short Vowels
2. The FLOSS and CK Rule

Schuler Phonics and Companion Books
WHERE "Sound it out" really works!

But to help it work, note the following:

Any word _italicized_/_underlined_ in these stories should NOT be sounded out --- because sounding out just won't work on those words! (A, a, The, the will not be italicized/underlined even though considered "non-phonetic"; there are just too many of them, and they really are not a problem!)

Note: "Sound it out" doesn't always work --- because there are lots of words that can't be sounded out unless a person knows "millions and millions" of phonetic rules.

Why Schuler Phonics works: Schuler Phonics only teaches the basic, most common rules and then uses words based on those rules, all of which then can be sounded out.

For the stories in this book collection your child should learn the following words by sight: _of_, The, the, and _to_ plus A, a, _and_, _box_, _fix_, _fox_ (phonics concepts not yet introduced). All the other words can be sounded out as they are based on short vowel and single consonant words, including the single phonetic consonant sound made by ff, ll, ss, zz, and ck. Note: The letter x in box, fix, and fox is not considered a single consonant sound because it makes two sounds /k/ and /s/ joined.

www.parentreadingcoach.org
FOR TRAINING VIDEOS

<u>IMPORTANT NOTE FOR PARENTS/TEACHERS</u>:

<u>A</u> or <u>a</u> should NOT be pronounced as long a (/ā/ as in the word say) in the phrase such as, "<u>A</u> hen, an egg, <u>a</u> cap." Instead, <u>A</u> or <u>a</u> should be pronounced as a short u (/ŭ/ as in umbrella /ŭ/ or up /ŭ/).

The e in the words <u>**The**</u> or <u>**the**</u> should NOT be pronounced as long e (/ē/ as in the word bee) in the phrase such as "<u>**The**</u> Big Egg." Instead the e in <u>**The**</u> or <u>**the**</u> should be pronounced as a short u (/ŭ/ as in umbrella /ŭ/ or up /ŭ/).

CONTENTS

STORY 1: DOLCH SIGHT WORDS

The Big Egg

Gloria Torres

COMPANION STORY 1: DOLCH SIGHT WORDS

Non-phonetic Dolch sight words:
The   the

Phonetic Dolch sight words (But phonics concept not yet introduced):
A   a

Dolch vocabulary to practice:

an	hen	pig
bell	his	red
big	hot	sit
but	if	top
can	in	up
cap	is	well
cat	it	will
did	let	
dog	man	
duck	not	
egg	off	
get	on	
got	pick	

A hen, an egg, a cap.

The egg is big. The egg is hot. The hen got off the egg. The hen got the egg in a red cap.

The cat will get up on the egg. The cat will sit on top, but the egg will get hot. The cat will get off it.

The dog will get up on the egg. The dog will sit on top, but the egg will get hot. The dog will get off it.

The pig got up. The pig will get on the egg. The man will pick up the egg.

The man did not let the pig sit on the egg. The man will get his duck.

If the duck can sit on the egg, it will not get hot. The duck is on the egg. The egg is well.

Questions to check:

1. The egg is _____.
   a.   red
   b.   big
   c.   on

2. The egg is in a _____.
   a.   cap
   b.   can
   c.   bell

3. _____ will sit on the egg.
   a.   The man
   b.   The cat
   c.   The pig

4. _____ can not sit on the egg.
   a.   The pig
   b.   The duck
   c.   The dog

5. The egg is not hot if _____.
   a.   the pig will sit on it
   b.   the duck will sit on it
   c.   the dog will sit on it

STORY 2: DOLCH SIGHT WORDS

The Hen Egg

Mark Torres

COMPANION STORY 2: DOLCH SIGHT WORDS

Non-phonetic Dolch sight words:

The   the   _to_

Phonetic Dolch sight words (BUT phonics concept not yet introduced):

A   a

Phonetic words (but not Dolch):

hat   sat

Dolch vocabulary to practice:

an	get	on
bus	hen	pick
but	hill	pig
can	hot	red
cat	if	run
cut	in	sit
did	is	sun
dog	it	up
duck	man	will
egg	not	yes

The egg can get hot if it is in the sun.

But the egg is not in the sun. The egg is on the bus.

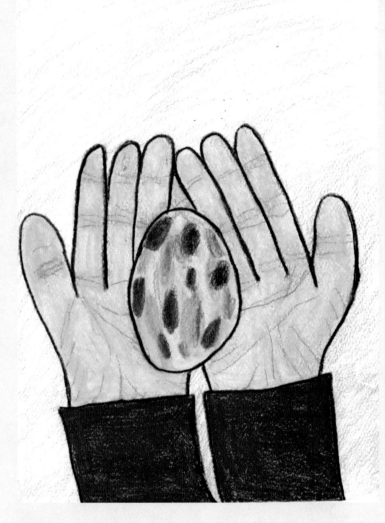

The man will sit on the bus. The man will pick up the egg.

"Is it a dog egg? A dog is not in an egg."

"Is it a duck egg? A duck is in an egg. Yes? Yes. Yes!"

The man will get the egg _to_ the duck. The duck is on a hill.

The man will run up the hill. The man did get the egg _to_ the duck. The duck sat on the egg.

"Man! It is not a duck egg. It is a hen egg."

Questions to check:

1. The egg is _____.
   a.   red
   b.   hot
   c.   cut

2. The egg is _____.
   a.   on the bus
   b.   in a can
   c.   on a hat

3. The egg is a_____.
   a. dog egg
   b. pig egg
   c. hen egg

4. _____ will pick up the egg.
   a.   The man
   b.   The cat
   c.   The pig

5. _____ will sit on the egg.
   a.   The pig
   b.   The duck
   c.   The dog

STORY 3: DOLCH SIGHT WORDS

The Pig Is Not His Pet

Gloria Torres

COMPANION STORY 3: DOLCH SIGHT WORDS

Non-phonetic Dolch sight words:
of   The   the

Phonetic Dolch sight words (BUT phonics concept not yet introduced):
A   a

Phonetic words (but not Dolch):
mud   pet   rat   sad

Dolch vocabulary to practice:

at	got	off
back	has	on
bed	hill	pick
bell	him	pig
big	his	ran
bus	hot	red
can	in	sit
cap	is	sun
cat	let	ten
dog	man	up
duck	men	will
get	not	

Ten men sit on the big bus. The red bell is at the back of the bus in a can. The man is at the back of the bus.

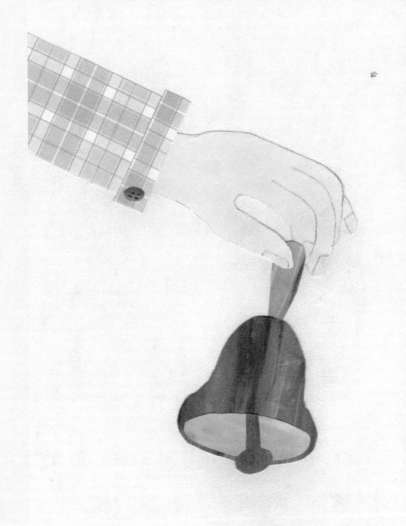

The man will pick up the bell. The bell is on.

The bus let the man off at the hill. The man got his pet cat. The man ran off the hill.

The sun is hot. The man is hot. The man can get on his cap.

The cat is hot.

The man will pick up his cat. The man will get a cap on his cat.

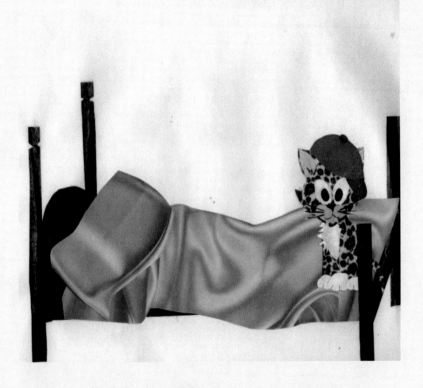

The cat has a cap. The cat is not in the sun. The cat is not hot. The cat is his pet. The man will let the cat on the bed.

The dog is hot.

The man will get a cap on his dog.

The man will pick up his dog.

The dog has a cap. The dog is not in the sun. The dog is not hot. The dog is his pet. The man will let him on the bed.

The duck is hot.

The man will get a cap on his duck.

The man will pick up the
duck.

The duck has a cap. The duck is not in the sun. The duck is not hot. The duck is his pet. The man will let the duck on the bed.

The pig is hot. The man will not pick up the pig.

The man will not let the pig get a cap. The man will not let the pig on the bed. The pig is big. The pig has mud.

The pig can not get on
the bed. The pig is sad.
The pig is not his pet.

Questions to check:

1. The _____ sit on the bus.
    a.   ten men
    b.   dog
    c.   cat
2. The sun is _____.
    a.   cap
    b.   hot
    c.   big
3. The man will get a cap on his _____.
    a.   dog
    b.   rat
    c.   pig
4. The man will let the _____ on the bed.
    a. duck
    b. rat
    c. pig
5. The man will not let the _____ sit on the bed.
    a. pig
    b. duck
    c. dog

STORY 4: PHONICS

Bob <u>and</u> His Dog, Ted

Theresa Torres

COMPANION STORY 4: PHONICS

Non-phonetic Dolch sight words:
The   the

Phonetic Dolch sight words (BUT phonics concepts not yet introduced):
a   _and_

Phonetic vocabulary to practice:

bad	in	up
bed	is	wet
Bob	kid	
can	mud	
cat	nap	
dog	off	
dug	on	
fed	pet	
fell	pets	
fun	pit	
got	pug	
had	ran	
has	sad	
hat	sun	
hill	Ted	
his	tub	

Bob is a kid.

Bob has a hat.

Bob got a pet.
The pet is a dog.

The dog is a pug.

The dog is Ted.

Ted dug a pit.
Ted is a bad dog.

The hat fell in the pit.

Bob is sad.

The dog, Ted, got the hat in the pit.

Bob fed his dog, Ted.

Ted had a nap on his dog bed. The dog, Ted, got up.

Ted ran up a hill. Ted fell in the mud.

The dog, Ted, got in the tub. Ted got wet. Ted got the mud off.

Bob had fun in the sun.
His dog, Ted, had fun in
the sun.

Questions to check:

1. Bob is a _____.
   a. kid
   b. cat
   c. dog
2. Ted is a _____.
   a. kid
   b. cat
   c. pug
3. Ted dug a _____.
   a. kid
   b. hill
   c. pit
4. The _____ fell in the pit.
   a. can
   b. hat
   c. dog
5. The dog fell in _____.
   a. the pit
   b. the mud
   c. the can

STORY 5: PHONICS

The Duck <u>and</u> the <u>*Fox*</u>

Mark Torres

COMPANION STORY 5: PHONICS

Non-phonetic Dolch sight words:
The   the   <u>to</u>

Phonetic Dolch sight words (BUT phonics concepts not yet introduced): a   <u>and</u>   <u>box</u>

Phonetic words, not Dolch (BUT phonics concepts not yet introduced):
<u>fox</u>

Phonetic vocabulary to practice:

an	had	off
at	has	on
back	hat	pen
bad	hid	pig
bed	hill	ram
big	his	ran
can	hit	rob
cap	in	sad
den	is	sat
did	leg	tell
duck	lick	up
egg	mad	will
get	nap	yak
got	not	yes

The duck had an egg in a <u>box</u>.

The duck sat on the big egg.

The _fox_ hid. The duck got off the egg.

The duck had a nap.

The bad _fox_ will rob the egg. The duck is sad.

The duck ran <u>to</u> the pig. The pig is in the pen. The pig will not tell the duck yes. The pig did not rob the egg.

The duck ran up the hill <u>to</u> the yak. The yak will not tell the duck yes. The yak did not rob the egg.

The duck ran <u>to</u> the ram. The <u>fox</u> has the egg. The ram will tell the duck yes.

The mad ram hit the _fox_ on the leg. The _fox_ did lick his leg. The _fox_ ran.

The ram got the big egg
back _to_ the duck. Yes,
the big egg is back!

The duck will nap on the egg in the _box_.

The _fox_ is in his den. The _fox_ did not get the egg.

Questions to check:

1. The egg is in a _____.
   a. hat
   b. cap
   c. box

2. _____ will rob the egg.
   a. The fox
   b. The ram
   c. The yak

3. _____ is mad at the fox.
   a. The pig
   b. The ram
   c. The yak

4. The ram hit the _____.
   a. duck
   b. pig
   c. fox

5. The duck will nap on _____.
   a. the egg
   b. the bed
   c. the can

STORY 6: PHONICS

The Cub Has a Hat

Theresa Torres

COMPANION STORY 6: PHONICS

Non-phonetic Dolch sight words:
The   the

Phonetic Dolch sight words (BUT phonics concepts not yet introduced):
A   a   _box_

Phonetic words, not Dolch (BUT phonics concepts not yet introduced):
fix

Phonetic vocabulary to practice:

at	hat	not
bat	his	on
bed	hog	rat
bit	hug	rip
bus	in	rug
cat	is	sad
cub	kiss	tuck
den	mad	up
get	mop	well
got	mud	will
has	nap	

A cub is in his den.
The cub has a hat.

A rat bit the hat.
The cub got mad.

The rat will _fix_ the hat.
The cub is not mad.

A cat will rip the hat.
The cub will get mad.

The cat will _fix_ the hat.
The cub is not mad.

A hog will get mud on the hat. The cub got mad.

The hog will mop up the mud. The cub is not mad.

The cat will hug the cub
in his bed. The cub will
nap well.

The hog will tuck the cub in his bed. The cub will nap well.

The rat will kiss the cub in his bed. The cub will nap well.

The cub will nap well in his bed in his den.

Questions to check:

1. The cub is in a _____.
     a. box
     b. den
     c. bus

2. The _____ bit the hat.
     a. rat
     b. cub
     c. cat

3. The _____ is mad at the rat.
     a. cat
     b. hog
     c. cub

4. The cat will rip the _____.
     a. bed
     b. hat
     c. rug

5. The _____ will kiss the cub.
     a. rat
     b. hog
     c. bat

Glossary

Dolch/Sight Words: Words your child should <u>first</u> sound out, using phonics, and then master by sight, so sounding out is no longer necessary.

Phonics: A practice of sounding out words.

Consonants: Sounds, phonemes, which are blocked by the teeth, tongue, and/or lips. Sometimes it is just easiest to think of consonants as all the letters that are not vowels: b, c, d, f, g, h, j, k, l, m, n, p, q, r, s, t, v, w, x, y (y can be a vowel or a consonant), and z.

Vowels: Sounds, phonemes, which are NOT blocked when pronounced. The vowels are a, e, i, o, u, and sometimes y.

Short Vowels: /a/ as in apple, /e/ as in elephant or Ed, /i/ as in igloo or itch, /o/ as in octopus, and /u/ as in umbrella or up.

CK Rule: The sound of /k/ can be spelled with c, k, or ck. After a short vowel, the /k/ sound is spelled with a ck.

Floss Rule: The /f/ sound can be spelled with f or ff; the /l/ sound can be spelled with l or ll; the /s/ sound can be spelled with s or ss, and the /z/ sound can be spelled with s, z or zz. After a short vowel /f/ is spelled ff, /s/ is spelled ss, /l/ is spelled ll, and /z/ is spelled zz. Those two letters (ff, ll, ss, zz) still only make one sound.

ABOUT THE AUTHORS

Gloria Torres and Theresa Torres are middle school twins who love to write and draw. Mark is in high school. He likes the arts and sciences and inventing. Nicholas is in high school. He enjoys lifeguarding and working with computers. They all play soccer and live in Los Alamos, New Mexico.

Answer Key

The Big Egg
1. The egg is **b) big**.
2. The egg is in a **a) cap**.
3. **b) The cat** will sit on the egg.
4. **a) The pig** can not sit on the egg.
5. The egg is not hot if **b) the duck will sit on it**.

The Hen Egg
1. The egg is **b) hot.**
2. The egg is **a) on the bus.**
3. The egg is a **c) hen egg.**
4. **a) The man** will pick up the egg.
5. **b) The duck** will sit on the egg.

The Pig is Not His Pet
1. The **a) ten men** sit on the bus.
2. The sun is **b) hot**.
3. The man will get a cap on his **a) dog**.
4. The man will let the **a) duck** on the bed.
5. The man will not let the **a) pig** sit on the bed.

Answer Key - Continued

Bob and His Dog Ted
1. Bob is a **a) kid**.
2. Ted is a **c) pug**.
3. Ted dug a **c) pit**.
4. The **b) hat** fell in the pit.
5. The dog fell in **b) the mud**.

The Duck and the Fox
1. The egg is in a **c) box**.
2. **a) The fox** will rob the egg.
3. **b) The ram** is mad at the fox.
4. The ram hit the **c) the fox**.
5. The duck will nap on **a) the egg.**

The Cub Has a Hat
1. The cub is in a **b) den**.
2. The **a) rat** bit the hat.
3. The **c) cub** is mad at the rat.
4. The cat will rip the **b) hat.**
5. The **b) hog** will kiss the cub.

Made in the USA
Middletown, DE
19 October 2022